A Brief Description

There was nothing to suggest anything out of the ordinary as I got in my car to drive to the local town for food supplies, but this drive turned out to be anything but ordinary. As a shamanic healer I am accustomed to communicating with my spirit guides as easily as interacting with friends and clients, so much so that when Merlin started to engage in a conversation while I was driving, it was as if I was talking with someone in the passenger seat, as the legendary Merlin began to talk to me about producing this work that I would channel from him. The seed of this book was sown during that short car drive, an extraordinary few moments that were above and beyond the normal run to the shops and which began a magical, deeply priveleged collaboration.

The result is a powerful, eloquent guide to help answer the great perrenial questions and support the challenges of life we all face at some time. Challenges that cause difficulties, suffering and confusion about what life is about, who we are and what our purpose in life is. It is a guide to help bring awareness of your own unique gifts and strengths so you may fully express their potential. To be able to break free from self doubt and conditioning and allow your a‎ self to blossom

This is an empov
is direct but witl
softness about it

GW00694548

There are a lot of pauses and repeated words to emphasise points and if it is read with that in mind, allowing the energy of the words to really connect with your own energy, it becomes a form of meditative reading, creating a deep connection with the self.

It is a guide for embracing and fully living your life, it is not imparting a doctrine, it is simply a guidance system, a support mechanism for You To Be All that You Can Be.

Published by SoulConnection

Copyright © Martin Robbins 2014

Printed in Ireland - Prisma Print Limited. (Cork)

A Concise Guide To A Life On Earth

Love, Support, Empowerment and Inspiration from Merlin

Directly Channelled by Martin Robbins

Martin Robbins BSc (Hons.) Psychology
Shaman - Artist
Workshop Facilitator of Shamanic Practice
One 2 One Shamanic Healing and
Counselling Sessions

Author of "Shamanic Soul Connection",
Boxset containing 24 Animal Image cards,
48 page book and a CD of drumming for the
shamanic journey

Published by SoulConnection

Copyright © Martin Robbins 2014

Printed in Ireland - Prisma Print Limited. (Cork)

ISBN 9780993098000

How To Use This Book

As well as reading from cover to cover, this book serves as a powerful divination tool and can be read very much like a set of divination cards. Hold the book in your hands and sit quietly for a few moments. Think of a number between 1 and 20 and one will flash through your mind perhaps followed by another. The first number that appears is the number of the chapter in the book that holds the key to the questions you have. Read this chapter first followed by the chapter corresponding with the second number if there was one. This second chapter serves as a strengthening and a confirmation of the information given in the first chapter you read.

Contents

Introduction

I first had the honour of Merlin's presence during shamanic practitioner training with The Sacred Trust in 2007/8. During the second half of the training there were 3 occasions when I was chosen to "become" Merlin for an octet healing session. One of the group members received healing from 8 helpers who were all given the privelege to "take on" the spirit of one of our teachers own spirit guides. When the process was complete, each one of us was taken over by a guide who could then have the human experience and speak through the recipient. Merlin gave the diagnosis for each healing and the others had roles which helped to impart the work.

It was made clear to me early on in my training that I should use my artistic skills in a shamanic way although at the time I didn't know how or in what shape that would take. The idea was put on the back burner while I immersed myself in the work of becoming a shamanic healer. Eventually, I was in that place where creative ideas and passion flowed resulting in a set of cards depicting power animals. I then wanted to see if it was possible for me to draw the portraits of my spirit guides and I journeyed to Merlin to ask his permission and guidance. The result was the powerful image on the cover of this book which I have carried with me since those early days of shamanic experience.

Recently I had been listening to the work of Abraham

Hicks on youtube and one particular day was in my car driving along when I suddenly had the thought of how fabulous it must be to be the link between spirit and large audiences, conveying information that would help and inspire people to have the life that really expresses their unique gifts and potential. As soon as I had that thought Merlin appeared and asked me if I wanted to do it, I was very excited and in a nanosecond said yes. This was quickly followed by how and what questions, still driving along while a stream of dialogue flowed from Merlin on how it could be accomplished, starting with a book to introduce the work.

I was reticent as to whether I could, me, do this, but Merlin was persistent and reassured me that he would speak through me and I would be a channel for his words which would form the book. By the time I arrived home, the practicalities of this incredible project were sorted. Spirit allowed me a brief period of procrastination and then had me walking into a hifi shop and spontaneously buying a dictaphone without a seconds hesitation!

A neat shove in the back to get on with it!
Using my shamanic drumming cd, I began making 30 minute shamanic journeys to Merlin to receive each chapter. I always had no idea what each session would be about but after narrating the journey to Merlin's cave and meeting him, the words always flowed. I had felt strongly from the beginning that there would be twenty chapters and when I visited Merlin for the twentieth

session, I was struck dumbfounded once again at the magic that had unfolded, a perfect closing chapter wrapped up the work brilliantly.

Two weeks after starting this work, I found myself moving completely unplanned from Ireland to Glastonbury in the U.K. a place of special significance for Merlin and then equally unexpectedly, returning to Ireland when the work was finished. It was in Glastonbury I was to experience first hand All of the issues, situations and emotions that would be addressed in the book just prior to receiving the solutions and guidance from Merlin. This made sense to me but it still made for a very challenging time, however I believe I was being prepared by spirit to be able to speak the words of the different chapters when the time comes with integrity and true experience which would further enhance the message they bring.

When that is to happen rests again with spirit and I look forward to it.

This work has been a wonderful collaboration and I am deeply honoured to have been a part of it.

The framework is a no nonsense, eloquent and empowering guide to finding that fulfilment we all seek, finding our true self and expressing who we are in the world with all the unique qualities and gifts we each have. It's about taking back our spiritual power and truly living the life we came here to have.

The words have been delivered to you, direct from Merlin who resides in the invisible energy of spirit and knowledge that immerses everything.

I ask that you read the words as they are presented with all the pauses and emphases so that you may feel their energy connecting with yours, bringing you healing, resonance with your truth, understanding, richness and empowerment.

This is the Wish for You,
of Merlin, of Spirit

Chapter One

...About You

I'm at the tree, there are several figures there, the animals are at the base they're coming with me, running up the branches of the tree and the trunk of the tree as I go up. We are gathered on a ledge in the Upperworld, there's a spirit there guiding us, beckoning us to the path on the cliff. Wolf is there leading, Eagle is flying around, Stag, Owl is flying, Elephant is coming behind. We go round a corner, it's a very narrow path to a cavernous dark cave. A light is there from a lamp, and as I get closer, Merlin's face appears, the animals settle down, sitting down with me. "You have come", he says, "Yes Merlin I have come". "Are you ready to pass the information, pass the words, that will form the book"? "Yes I am".

Listening with the heart, what does that mean? It

can have all kinds of different meanings depending on how you are feeling in the moment. You can feel betrayed, you can feel joyous, expectant, surprised, or pain, until you realise Why you feel in the heart or how it is even possible for you to feel in the heart. What you feel in your mind, there won't be the healing or the understanding for you to trust that feeling and change that feeling if necessary. Your heart is the representative of your soul, it reflects the conflict between your soul and mind and body, your mind really, because a large percentage of your actions and thoughts come from your mind, your subconscious mind. Many of them are not in coherence with your true nature, your authentic self. The authentic self that is your spirit, your essence. You need to really realise this, this truth through your heart and body. Awareness of your thoughts, awareness of your actions, the incoherence of them with your heart, with your spirit, allows a little space to form and then a questioning, a questioning of their power because they have a power over you at that moment before the awareness, they are holding the power, they are controlling you and taking you away from the route the path that your authentic self wants to take. It is here, your authentic self is here to take you through life on a route that will allow you to experience and express the qualities and the potential you carry, the gifts, the abilities, the seeds of which are in you, they came with you into this life. The potentials and extraordinary qualities that will give you an abundant joyful life as you use your gifts to create and grow are the keys for you to manifest the life that your gifts, your power, came with you to give you during this time in this earthly body.

It is when we don't or can't listen, when we are so overwhelmed by the pressures and stresses of life that our subconscious mind and conditioning has allowed us to wrap around ourselves. We wrapped themselves around with restrictions and fears and the need for security, the need for answers and this need for answers and security has reduced our capacity for making the decisions that will enable the growth and abundant life we came here to have .

We have been sabotaging ourselves but we don't even know that, we can't know that, how can we know that with the restrictions and fears and suppressed frameworks for living that we received when we were young from our elders who were equally restricted and fearful, constrained and suppressed and reduced almost to a much of a robotic existence. Repeating behaviours and words like rote because they had completely lost their power their individual sense of self and their ability to discern what they really wanted for themselves in this life.

And so it has been for you until this moment, this moment of realisation, of beginning to realise the truth tool that you carry within. The authentic component, the pure component that is not confined by conditioning and fear. It is pure, free, powerful. Restriction isn't in it's vocabulary, freedom is, it's the main concern, freedom to be, freedom to be. We are taught we must do some certain things, behave in certain ways but all these things and ways are set by the very people confined by fear and restriction and without even being aware and knowing they continue that way of being into the next generation. Ask yourself what it feels like, what would it feel like, to know without doubt who you are, what you are capable of and that you can achieve what you desire regardless of the risks that are placed in front of you, the boundaries and the barriers. If you know that you can, by believing in yourself and by knowing yourself, trusting your authentic self that you can achieve your full potential, you can realise the potential you have whichever way you choose to use it. Not to wait until after 40 or 50 years of working and living in a way that is incoherent with your authentic self, retire from a lifetime of constraint and missed opportunities through fear and lost belief and by following the rules that govern a restricted way of being. Looking forward to the day when you retire from the work so that you may do what you want.When you look back on that life, youv'e been here for all that time and not taken the opportunities that have shown up that will allow you , lead you to express all that you can be. All the gifts that you brought with you have been suppressed in order to comply with fear.

There will be a lifetime of regret, you will look back and remember those occasions that presented themselves that appeared to be so exciting and resonated with your authentic self, something that would have enhanced your growth, your spirit, your self and launched you into a different direction in life bringing great fulfilment and abundance for your spirit, your heart, your self. But your conscious mind got in the way, your rational mind got in the way. It questioned, debated and questioned and the more your mind debated and questioned, the risk of change became greater. Until very quickly, the door was closed, the opportunity was lost, and the cloak of fear became thicker and stronger, and your heart, your authentic self became quieter.

Chapter Two

Heading Off Into Reality

You came from spirit, you came from spirit . You may have heard that a lot, but what does it mean? It means you came from the energies of the universe, energies that give life to all and everything in the universe, creating life, the physical matter of life. It brings together components of different energies that will be coherent with the energy that exists. The physical forms of the energies that exist and the energies that combine contain new elements and coexist with already physical forms bringing new elements to that existing potential to elevate, create and add new aspects to the energies. Some call it evolution, call it creativity, creatively developing what already exists. You came here as that form of energy, that combination of new energies that would add another layer, helping to add another layer of development to those that already existed. So you arrived with gifts and the ability to help extend the evolution. Everybody has talents and gifts and energies to do that. And it's our responsibilities, a responsibility more than anything to ourselves to the honouring of the source of life. We have been given an opportunity for a very short time, a comparatively very short time to make a small difference and experience the wonder of the experience. To share in the actualisation of all the other energies that come into our time through the other lives that we interact with. Then the possibilities of combining the energies, our energies and talents and potentials to create deeper layers of growth will have more impact and depth to the evolution that is constantly taking place.

Abuse and violence, the ego, the negative consequences of power can destroy the individual potentials of many, many people and there is a constant battle, a constant conflict for the authentic self to express its true nature without fear or ego. There's a constant threat to the self to comply to the wishes of the powers and energies of others. So it is that the evolution that is possible for new generations who arrive with their unique qualities to enhance growth of what already exists is reduced and the endless battle of conditioning and restriction and fear, limitations, doubts and expectations of failure continues. The need to belong is a powerful force that takes away individual authentic power and replaces it with subconscious disempowerment. Many times we don't know we are disempowered, we think we are living our life the way we should, the lives we came here to live and we complain and get frustrated. Or we can even believe that we have no power, we have no say in our life, we just exist, this is our life for this moment and then we're gone like specks of dust blowing in the wind back into the universe.

What a terrible loss, what a terrible loss of potential, joy and excitement, experience, creative fulfilment and positive evolution. If we can somehow recognise or if we can begin to believe that there actually is more available to us in this life, and that we have the power, the key to that something with no reliance on other people events or anything. We brought it with us it's always been with us. If there is awareness of that, what a change, that opening to authenticity, that opening a door to your authentic self will bring to the identity that you carry from the life that you have had. It could be examined like an observer, objectively, looking at the life that you've had and the one you wanted at one point when you were still young enough to have dreams and desires before they were lost in the wind, in the wind of fear, winds of self-doubt and the expectations and beliefs, the negative beliefs of those around you. They are in your life because your energies were the same, you attracted each other. The same as everything is reflected back to you, what you believe about yourself, who you believe yourself to be, everything is a reflection of those beliefs.

This realisation can be huge, it could be rationally argued that it doesn't exist because the power that is behind the rational thought has been given the energy of evolution too with much more support and therefore stronger, deeper. And so there is a real conflict, there's a real battle which has to be slowly changed not in any way slowly changed but by awareness, and willingness to accept the new ideas. Your authentic self will quickly respond and you will know, you will change because you will know this is right, that this is right, this is the way to be, the way to live. Energy can balance your life in this world by you being authentic to yourself and being your truth and living in your truth. And participating fully, fully engaged in the life that you lead but with a different energy, the energy of engagement, the energy of knowing, of expectation, anticipation and excitement of new things and of what you will be able to do and of what you want to do. Awareness of your power and that you are participating in the evolution of all that exists by being here now with your gifts and potentials will help to allow the expression of those things, that is your life's task and in doing so your authentic self, your soul your spirit your mind your body will be fulfilled, will be abundant.

Go back in time to your childhood or maybe your teenage times, when you had dreams, when you had real great ideas for yourself and what life should be like. Go back when your authentic self, your true nature was able to express itself through thoughts, words and excited anticipation. Think of the times when you knew, you knew what was happening in your life was wrong, it didn't fit your truth, it didn't fit with your expectation of your journey it didn't resonate your essence, your spirit, your heart.

Chapter Three

When It Gets Tough

Straight along the ledge into the cave, Merlin is sitting there in the lamplight. "Welcome", he says. I sit , by a small fire.

Inner struggle, is not the intention, of the universe for your spirit. It wasn't the intended experience. The experience is about acceptance, acceptance of where you are in the world, the situation that you may find yourself in whatever situation it maybe, accepting it for what it is and allowing it, using it to be the springboard, for your growth. Utilising the experience and lessons, the conditions. Accept it how it is and see it as a kind of puzzle to find a solution to move from that situation. Have awareness of your desires, your dreams, the direction that you want to take your gifts, how you want to use the ability that you have.With that awareness and trust your ability will take you into a new environment in which your soul, your essence will thrive because it's like a seed germinating, sitting in the ground during the cold winter deep in the dark Earth and waiting for the moment when it is time to move, to begin to move to find its way in the darkness through the soil around the stones, wending its way through the weeds and the roots, continually holding on to its truth that it has beautiful potential to express in the world and have an important contribution to make in the continuation of life. You have a role to play, we all have a role to play and we need to find the route that will take us through the darkness and into the light. We can do that if we know, it's beyond belief it's a knowing, you just know, when you just know yourself, your purpose, your role.

Not purpose and role to go through the prescribed education system, choose a career a job and spend your life in that job or career and raise a family, it's beyond that, your role is beyond that. Those things are a part, they're a part of the whole reasoning for you to be here they are not the totality because alongside those things, your spirit has come here to explore and expand itself through experience and growth, creative growth, creative expansion and not to be subdued and caged in a life a way of life created by others. That's not to say, avoid that kind of life, have that kind of life but remember, it's remembering and really connecting, remembering your true nature, your true nature of desire and what it takes for that desire and your true nature what it wants in order to become, and embrace the beauty of life on this planet. It is so important, we are not our minds, we are not what our minds have created, we are not what other minds have created, that is not who we are so we don't want to be dominated by those principals.

We are individuals, we live with other people, we interact with other people, we work and engage with other people but our essential being, our essential being needs to be recognised and honoured and allowed to follow the opportunities that present for it to develop through the experiences to realise the potential within. It's essential that the mind steps aside so that the voice within can be heard and listened to, trusted, and followed. And then the mind becomes a support, the mind can become a support for our essential being, making rational choices in support of our true nature, prioritising those rational choices in support of our true nature, leading to partnership of growth without fear or doubt. Doubt and fear are eradicated, they don't exist, all that exists is this powerful partnership with one plan, the task of exploring all possibilities that present, with the freedom to change and change again. Change directions as different energies flow into our consciousness along with creative ideas leading to expansion, continuous expansion and fulfilment, engagement with not what we are just capable of doing but what we would like to do, what we dream to do.

And as ideas flow to us as we grow and open, we stay open and embrace the new energies, new ideas, new directions. Our heart remains open like somebody standing in a doorway, open and welcoming in visitors without restriction, knowing that some will not like it, there won't be the resonance from the surrounding energies to keep them there, they move on to where they do resonate, so that with an open mind and open heart there will be a life of adventure.

Chapter Four

When You Don't Listen

So,

....

....

....

....

....

....

*I*f you are in a situation in your life, a situation of stuckness, and this situation is so overwhelming with difficulty and pain, and the people closest to you are feeding the situation they are feeding that situation with the beliefs of themselves, limiting beliefs held within. It is draining, it drains our power without us knowing. There is no way out, we cannot see a wayout, this is what life, this is what my life is for, this is what it's about, nothing can change this, it is the way it is and I have to accept it. This kind of thinking makes a good survival plan and we may not even know we are making a survival plan, we may not be aware of our subconscious desires of change. All these layers of self-doubt, acceptance of what is have coated our spirit, it's camouflaged, it's subdued, we go about life with no reference to it or little reference to it, life is what presents itself in the now. This is life, this is here, this is the experience I'm having, this is my life.

Don't give up on yourself, don't give up on yourself. Remember your innocent childhood games, dreams. Perhaps there is no space for those dreams those games, if fear was the overriding experience. Somewhere deep within us right in the core of who we really are, is sending out a tiny signal to you a tiny voice of support, and the tiniest inkling that something else could be possible for you besides this. It has been there, it has always been there, it came with you ,it will never leave you even for the time that you leave it, it will always be there regardless, sending out it's signal even if it's the tiniest bleep, tiniest pulse of energy through the depths of your fear, and your limiting beliefs. In the darkest moments, of despair, of grief, there is an opening it's a crack, it's a crack through your defences which allows a momentary glimpse a momentary spark for the energy of the soul to filter through and give support and love to you. And the crack can get wider if we can open ourselves up and cry, and sob, pray, releasing the tension of the situation releasing the end of the energy of that tension through our tears and sobs, there's an opportunity of calm and connection with the force within you, the power within you.

Those waiting to support and help you, the warmth of the unconditional love may be felt momentarily because we are in such despair with feelings of hopelessness that our resources cannot perceive more than a momentary glimpse. If you can find the strength and resolve, resources, go within, go deep within yourself and beyond, beyond your beliefs and fears and there we find an ally. Whose concern for you is that you can go beyond that which is visible and strengthen the resolve, to listen to the new possibilities. To listen closer to that stronger, growing voice within you without conflicting, without conflict your rational mind becomes stronger and more resilient in imagining what could be. Dreaming of the possibilities for yourself, your authentic self and having the courage and strength to move from your situation of despair which offers security, a form of security, familiarity and identity to move from there to a new strange place that doesn't contain the same energies, but offers a new space for you to become, for you to truly become and bring about a joyful transformation.

It takes a lot of courage and strength to do that, but with the solid, always present support within you encouraging you, helping you to see how the possibilities of imagination of a new way of being, is a possibility that becomes your new reality, it can become your new reality.

Chapter Five

Love Is The Answer

At the tree, facing the tree looking up, I look up and the branches go to the sky, it's almost like they're breaking through the sky, and I find myself whooshing up very quickly up the branches, there's a kind of hole in the blue sky, into the blackness beyond. I land on the cliff, the familiar cliff, there's a familiar pathway that leads to Merlin's cave. The light from the candle or lamp is there. "Merlin, it's good to see you again after this time, the last few days have been amazing, great change, shift, opportunities, help and support, I offer my humble thanks.

And it's like this, opportunities come about, all the time in fact. Some are here very fast they come in and go, fleeting glimpses and clues to opportunities but we are so distracted in our everyday life we don't notice them or we don't see the significance of them. They come and go and disappear as fast as they arrived. And it's funny but it's after, usually after they've come and gone offering the very thing we have asked for, as soon as they've gone what we have an idea for, or a yearning for, the opportunity that would have brought that about and help manifest it has gone. It takes awareness, mindfulness of ourselves and our world, our reality, to notice these things.

Some are very subtle and although profound they are not standing in front of you like neon lights flashing shouting look at me, look at me, listen, take notice of this. Your heart doesn't need that marketing, that advertising, all it needs is the resistance that surrounds it to dissipate and allow that little crack, allow that little crack to allow that light to shine in into your heart. Because your heart is so powerful, your heart organ is powerful with it's strong electromagnetic waves it will then let the brain know, your mind know, of this opportunity. So it's about awareness, it's about awareness of yourself and how your heart is feeling, how your spirit is feeling, noticing your spirit emotions it's almost emotions of the spirit and how that is feeling. Not every moment of the day but allowing that subtle response to be felt and heard when it happens. Sometimes all it takes is to sit quietly, but that takes patience, it takes patience and allowing the knowing that's deep inside you to be heard, this is what is necessary for you to to meet the opportunity that is waiting for you. You can take a while, a while for that to happen, in our mind we have our ideas of how quickly it should take place, how simple things should be if theyr're going to be right for us.

We don't expect difficulty, we don't think there's going to be difficulty in identifying, for our spirit to identify what is right for us but in doing that and thinking in that way, we are putting a barrier around our spirit, our heart. Only allowing in what we think, because our mind is taking over, and filtering out the essence of what is waiting, the truth of what is waiting. So our mind can take control and we get frustrated and we get fed up, and we get depressed and we get annoyed or we just give up, we just give up waiting and go on to something else. Some other distraction that is new and exciting and interesting, but just for a short time because however interesting and exciting and attractive it may be it isn't the truth, it isn't your truth. And so you can go from one thing to another easily and quite happily in the illusion that what is happening, what you're experiencing is your truth, or perhaps not even that it's just exciting, just interesting, and it takes you away from your perhaps normal mundane life for a short while. Or maybe the ideas are coming in of what the future may hold for you if you do certain things, particular things, feelings of what you should be doing, that will enable you to reach your desire. So the mind can dictate your truth for you, if you're not careful and mindful. But the source of your truth isn't in your mind, it's in your heart. And so we wait, and wait, perhaps so intent on waiting envisioning the route we should be taking and waiting for that to manifest.

Little cracks of lights appear, little cracks of opportunities appear that perhaps don't immediately present themselves as routes to that opportunity, so we allow our mind to dismiss them, that's not good enough for us, that's not going to help, that's not what I want to do. But it's the mindset forcing that thinking, a change of thinking will change everything, a change of mindset from negativity to positivity. Thinking outside the box, perceiving it from a different angle, giving it a different attitude, and perhaps the the magic of this opportunity will begin to shine. It will begin to generate not just a stream of rational thought towards it but also that feeling in your heart when it resonates with the vibration of the moment, because the moment is now bringing to you your truth and the energy of that opportunity. The shift in the perception of that opportunity has made the difference between mind dominated negative thought and positive heartfelt truth. When you embrace this, when you allow that moment to happen, the very act of doing so, increases vibrational resonance to open the doors to the barriers that may need to be crossed en route to the opportunity. And the energy of those barriers then dissipates and support arrives from spirit in order to make that happen, breaking down the barriers, making the opportunity accessible as you accept, as you accept the presence of the opportunity in your life.

This is the first step in the domino effect of breaking down the barriers, the opportunity to manifest. And as the barriers fall, your heart, accepts the opportunity that is unravelling easily before you, as your truth, your true opportunity that will enable you to reach your goal, your desire. Everything that you've been asking for from your heart, yearning for, waiting for, has been sitting waiting for this moment so that it can begin to manifest. That can only happen, if there is the feeling of belief in your heart, the acceptance of belief will send out the resonance, the energetic resonance that will allow those things to appear. Those things that have been waiting for you, just as you've been waiting for them and all that it's taken is the waiting to be finished, the waiting to be over. It's your belief, the power of belief that lies in your heart. The power of the heart over your mind, clearing your mind of needs and frustrations and desires and wants and needs and desires in exchange for waiting and trusting and knowing that the power of belief is the only language.

Chapter Six

Life Changes, Get Used To It

Standing at the tree, straight into the Upperworld, along the path and into the cave, he's very pleased to see me, in the candlelight I take a seat. "It's been a while, there's some important things to say,"

Just imagine, your life as a clean plate. a clean slate, a palette of different colours, all the colours that are available are there for you, on this plate, for you to use or mix together in whatever combination, feels right for you. That you can create whatever reality you wish to have with this palette of colours, it's entirely up to you to choose. This is the way of all things , this is the way that was given to you as you came, when you decided that it was time for you to return to earth, to return to this great adventure to explore, experiment and experience a range, a vast range of different elements of life on Earth in physical form. You arrived with your selected palette, your brushes and your pad, ready to embark on this creative journey with a whole project in mind of what you wanted to achieve with what you had chosen to do. But the critics that came your way tried to steer you in a different direction, pointing out your faults, your weaknesses and making suggestions that would improve your work, and gradually, subtley you began to engage in others adventures, working with other palettes of colours and some resonated with yours and some didn't. It is time to find your palette, your colour, the colours that represent who you are, what your dreams are for yourself and if others carry the same dream your paths will cross along the way. And for others whose dreams don't resonate with yours it is time to erase them from your work , your artbook, your artbook of life and so you stay with your own style, your own style of working, your own style of being. By doing so you discover the joy and immense satisfaction and fulfillment in being, your own master of your own work, and when other people look at your work, some will be in awe, of wonder at the beauty you have created yourself. The wonderful resonating assembly that is your life. And others will be judgemental and critical because your work doesn't resonate with theirs and that is their journey, their adventure, an adventure of different colours to yours. When you accept, the grace of your life, when you believe that you are the master of your life, great fulfilment and self-esteem and confidence will grow within you giving you new dimensions and avenues and opportunities to further express the pureness of you. This is why you are here, this is why you are here, to engage, in exploring the full potential of your creativity of whatever form that may take whatever colour it may have. It is a responsibility to yourself for you to follow, that path that idea, that creative thought that nags at you in your mind for you to explore further. Some will be difficult to accomplish, the challenges that face you can be great, because as you move along your route, you'll be constantly challenged and stretched beyond your comfort zone to confront your fears, your limitations and doubts. But as you push yourself further and further through these challenges, you will be more empowered. You'll know what it feels like to be, to accomplish, what you are capable of doing what you came here to do. So always, always, pay attention, to your colours to the colour of your palette and experiment with new permutations, challenges, mixes and extend yourself, extend yourself beyond your comfort, this is where the real joy of life emanates. The alternative is to stop creating, is to stop playing and mixing, experimenting, trying, reaching beyond that what you've done before and stay as you are in a safe place, in a familiar place and accept that what is, is all that there is. To do this is to deny yourself, deny yourself, because as you push yourself further, new opportunities, new creative visions, thoughts, ideas appear and you never know, you would never know without trying, without going further forward what is waiting, what is there to manifest as a reward for your endeavours. Your journey, will continue however you have mixed your colours, but the result depends on you. It depends on you because you have the final word, the final say in the creation of your own life, empowerment and fulfillment of your potential that you have brought with you to fully express. It's like arriving at a party with a bag full of drinks and food and going home early and returning home with a bag containing some drinks and food, returning home without fully expressing, not fully using the contents of your bag of potential. And so it gets lost, it gets forgotten, it goes mouldy and stale eventually thrown away. What a waste, of the journey, the possibilities of the journey have been wasted, have been cut short. At some point, as years go by, as time goes by, there will be reflection and possible sadness, regret, of what could have been. This is not what you are here for, this is not what you are here to experience, so just remember your palette of colours, a vibrant mix of who you are, the potential of what those colours can create, your colours can create and never give up. There are possibilities waiting for you to mix those colours into the masterpiece that will represent your life. And then you may look back and gaze upon this time and smile,

Chapter Seven

Darkness Can be A Friend Too

*T*he power animals are gathered round me by the tree, hoisting me up the tree, climbing the branches and then quickly stand up and come out onto the cliff, round the path into the cave. Merlin is sitting over a fire, the light of the fire reflects around the rocks, he smiles and beckons me in. "How you doing"? He says, "come and sit down, it looks like you need some comfort". He says,

You know there is nothing wrong with wanting some comfort in your life, it's perfectly natural to have familiar things around you, familiarity, structure, roots giving stability from which to, live and grow, develop, but you know sometimes we need to leave that behind us even for a short while and experience discomfort, dis-ease,uncertainty, even loneliness and fear of the future. When we feel these things, find ourself sinking into them we can comfort ourselves in the knowledge that everything changes, every thing changes, even the good times the strong times, the abundant times, the safe familiar times they are changing too in different ways. All the time we are experiencing them, because we are changing, all the time, and desires and dreams, perceptions shift, our priorities shift. There is a constant flow of movement within us and when we are feeling safe and familiar, comfortable, we don't notice, it's harder to notice the changes around us, within us. It's easier to notice the changes in other people but not within ourselves, even though they form the perception we have of our life as our life goes by. So when we find ourselves in that dark place, that unfamiliar place, that fearful place, that lonely place, we experience the full force of what change means, and if the changes are strong we forget that it is also part of the cycle of life and like everything in the cycle of life there is movement and change.

Within every period that we experience, we have the opportunity to appreciate, change our way of being, alter the way we are with just little perceptive shifts in different directions and sometimes those dark places are a bridge to those new directions. They can lead us, even force us to confront ourself, to confront ourself in a dark place, it can be a deep experience, a personal confrontation with our self something that might not be possible in a good light of life. And it's only by confronting our self in a dark place we find the strength, we find an inner strength, we adapt, we find our way to encourage ourselves to support our self.

But really what we're doing is communicating with our spirit, we are listening to our spirit possibly for the first time for a long time, and in doing that, our connection with our self, our spirit is strengthened. Our ability to listen to our self to know our self on a much deeper level evolves as a result. It allows, it allows us to break free, of the barriers that exist around us, barriers of fear and limitation and in doing so we find a way to adapt to the dark and to lead ourselves out of the dark. Because as we adapt, our strength develops, an inner strength develops, our connection with our own spirit helps that strengthening and it gives us determination, it gives us a guidance system. A system, a way of adapting to our situation that will take us out from this dark place, changing our perceptions of our physical situation. We are even deep healing the conditioned limitations we have been holding within us. When we reach the light, when we come back to the light, our physical situation may not have changed, but our inner situation has shifted so that we can begin to see, and feel, and think, in a more positive way. And perhaps it has changed, we have changed, something about us has changed, perhaps we've healed something, perhaps we've gained some strength. It will stay with us and we can use all of this experience, the dark experience, to create a new light, a new form of light.

Because as we are growing and shifting from the dark the strengthening that we're receiving, that we're developing, is bringing with it perhaps subtle perceptions of new things, new ideas, new routes to take that we haven't thought of before because we were comfortable and familiar in the previous light. And the curtains that came down over that light, are now revealing possibilities that were hidden before, hidden behind, conditioning and fears that we didn't know or weren't aware of that had influenced who we were, how we were in the world before. Think of the seed deep down in the dark Earth finding its way up through the soil to the light, that surge of life, that surge of energy expressing itself in a beautiful new growth in the light. Think of yourself as that seed finding your way through the darkness of the earth, moving constantly towards the light. That beautiful, flowering, new harvest that is waiting to, sprout, from you as you enter the light as you re-enter the light. Re-entering the light at a different time to the one you were in before and while you were in the darkness changes were happening too to all the conceivable elements of your life in that time. So nothing will stay the same, nothing will be the same.

Some will have changed and improved as they step into a new light, but some will have slipped back into a period of darkness for their new growth to manifest later on at a different time. So you will be able to blossom with a new surge of life and energy with a new light around you with a different interaction with your familiar space, your familiar environment because you're coming back to the light with new strengths and ideas, the results of the healings that have happened, the lessons that have taken place and your connection with your own spirit. And that connection can grow with you because it has shown itself to you, you have shown yourself to it, so as you step into the new light you bring with you a dependable, strong, authentic support that will stay with you and will be with you also if and when darkness returns for the next winter. Because that's all it is, a winter of darkness, it's a season and just as the seasons change, your winter will turn into spring and your spirit will, will be there to celebrate with you along with all the other new growth, that has come about during that time. And so the newness, the newness of everything is there helping to make the darkness, easier, perhaps even more exciting, it can be a positive time it can be seen as a positive time, a time of challenge, a game of challenges that you will experience, conquer, and move on.

Chapter Eight

Wishing You Were Here

Power animals are gathered round,
they're quite excited, there's an excited
energy, this time I fly on the back of
Eagle past the tree, Eagle brings me gently down
straight to the entrance of the cave. There's more
light around the entrance, there's a white light
sparkling from the rocks, and there's more light
inside the cave. Merlin is sitting there and he
actually looks younger, he is younger, he's
changed, he's wearing paler clothing, whiter
clothing, his beard is white. "Come and sit down",
he says. He's patting a rock for a seat, "how are
you feeling?" he asks. "Feeling tired, feeling tired
and a bit confused, around the lessons, for my
situation, the situation that I find myself in".

There's lessons to be learned in every situation,
and sometimes, it isn't clear what they are, so the
situation becomes a struggle, like a fog engulfing

and holding you in this kind of limbo space. But that is why the situation has arisen, because you need to go through this experience in order to, expose, those things that need to be addressed, and to perhaps really go deeply within, quiet moments, away from the distraction of the situation, away from distracting thoughts that fill the mind. Perhaps by taking a walk into nature, and being with the peace that it gives, a peace of balance to bring about an awakening. Allowing that space to be created that will allow new thoughts, new information, new clues, ideas to appear out of nowhere, out of no other memory or experience, purely and simply arriving fresh from the Universe that is guiding your journey and putting forward some guidance that will support.

And it's only in those quiet moments that, focus, an inner focus that these insights, can appear. It is important to write them down, it's important to write them down so that you can engage with them, engage with them by thinking them out, thinking around them what could they possibly mean? What are they saying to me? What are they giving me? What are they telling me?
Sometimes it will take some time, before it is possible to put together, thoughts and ideas, that

will not only change the situation but be a sustainable change, an exciting different approach, that wasn't available in the fog. And then sit with these thoughts, sit with the ideas but focus on them , this is the first stage, the first stage of beginning a new approach to changing the situation and moving into another one that will bring improvement, and change, perhaps it won't be physical, perhaps it'll be a change of perception, a small nudge or a movement of a different idea, a different approach to the same situation that will make that situation a very different place.

One that will, one that will bring about an acceptance, an acceptance of what is and what is happening and a way of working with that, and being with it. The acceptance can then grow into new ways into new tangents, into new pathways, a whole new different stream of thoughts, strategy can emerge because of your acceptance. Bringing about, a feeling of coping, of allowing, the situation to be, and in doing so, tremendous shifts can happen, tremendous shifts in the expectations and restricted outlook that might have been there before and which created this fog. And now the fog is lifting, it is lifting to reveal not just a different situation but a different you, a different you is emerging that will allow the situation to be, but which also allows you, to be, with it. The power of this acceptance, the power of what is, the power of accepting what is and working with it can be a powerful healing in itself. It can make us more grounded, more happy with ourselves and we find ways of adapting easier, we find ways to include those things that brought us joy that we have forgotten about, a way of inserting those things into our routine that was blocking any joyful experience. And we're able to find a way of combining the two elements and as we do so, our gratitude increases, our gratitude for the elements that bring us joy increases, gratitude for ourself.

A more empowered self has emerged. Even if it's just for a few moments, the fact that we can include those moments in our life is empowering, it empowers us and we know that we're not fully taken over by the situation. We can overcome it by continuing to do the things that bring us joy. We maybe urged to change our routine, a routine in which we were stuck but comfortable and which enabled us to operate, to a certain degree, but didn't resonate with who we actually are. It was there it was comfortable, it was a habit, and became more and more difficult to break. But when we start to change that routine, we can, have the things that truly resonate with us, deep within, the things that we are passionate about. Because although we were stuck in that routine of familiarity, and our habitual actions, our spirit was yearning for those moments of creativity that so resonate within us and bring joy. The first stage is to allow that crack of awakening, the stepping aside and allowing, a fresh input from spirit that has been waiting for that moment, to help the journey that you are on.

Whatever situation, whatever moment we find ourselves in however difficult, if we can detract from it for a few moments go into a quiet place in our minds, in our heart, to allow a space that crack to appear which will allow wisdom, the pure wisdom and guidance of the universe to flow through us. It is always there, available to us, waiting for that moment when our minds are quiet and our hearts are open, for those insights, the insights that it has for us, to be heard. The peaceful state of nature, the peaceful energy of nature is full of guidance and insights for us, we are surrounded by it and it contains answers that will lead us into new exciting spaces and pathways, experiences and situations, and all we need to do is accept and believe that it is available. We have this resource available to us all of the time, and each of us has access to it all of the time, and whenever, we ask with a clear mind and an open heart, it will answer.

Chapter Nine

Presence, The Greatest Gift

*T*he power animals are gathered at the base of the tree, I climb on their backs, they're crawling up the tree with me. Eagle comes down and I climb on his back, we fly, up into the darkness, there's a bright light coming from the cave which illuminates the cliff. Eagle settles down onto the ledge and I go into the brightly lit cave, Merlin is there, he smiles, offers me a seat. "Welcome ", he says.

It has taken you some time to get here today, it's an interesting journey you're having, full of ups and downs, intrigue, questions, fears and doubts, questioning. Always questioning, searching, as you push yourself through the search, of that elusive purpose, ask yourself what is that purpose? What is it that somehow holds the key to what I believe will be a life that I'm here to have? And as you ask that question, just reflect back on the experiences that you have had and the events that have taken place in your life, the happenings, the spontaneous unplanned surprises that brought about new experiences, meetings, and creativity. Just reflect on those for a moment and begin to realise that as you've been living your life you have been living your purpose all of this time, all of this time that you have been here has been reflecting purpose.

Everything, has arisen to bring you where you are now to this place, a place very different some time ago, a different you has emerged, and that's partly what your purpose is about, it's about growth and strength, focus, and movement, movement and change through life experiencing new things, pushing yourself through the barriers that restrict and confine your spirit. Constantly pushing back the barriers and allowing, creating, the space for the new to appear. It's a bit like having Winters hibernation, closing down and waiting and allowing to be whatever is occurring and when the time is right, when your work has been done and you're ready for the next Spring to bring forth fresh buds of inspiration, new directions, new ideas that brings about the next step for you. And if you are ready, it will show itself, when you are ready it will show itself. You'll be given signs, synchronicity will occur to bring about the helping hand of spirit, to manifest, the next step on your path that has been waiting for this moment for you to be ready to receive it.

Constant questioning, constant worrying and concerns, create the blocks to manifesting what you are actually after, what you want, what is waiting for you, it prevents the subtle signs being noticed, the subtle signs always there being given to you by spirit. And knowing this, give yourself a break, give yourself a rest from the constant, searching, constant unease and discontent that you may feel, because your purpose has never been quite clear. Perhaps the definition of your purpose, your perception of what that is needs to be looked at, examined, even questioned so that a different perspective can be achieved of the whole idea of what your purpose in life is. The skills and the gifts that you have with you, that you brought with you, are being given the opportunities to be expressed in different ways and different ways that you might imagine but they are being expressed. Perhaps it's time to have a look at those and see how they are supporting you in your life, appreciate them in your life, and rest in the knowledge that they are there with you, that you have them, they are yours, and they are your's in order that your purpose can be revealed whichever way, it may occur. Don't restrict perception of that purpose, because by restricting your perception of that purpose, you're restricting manifestation of the growth that will lead you to it, leading you through it and creating your life as you go.

This is your purpose, allowing the flow, of your life, to go where it needs to go, through all the cracks, of the rocks, the barriers that appear which can seem to be overwhelmingly difficult or just in the way, frustratingly stopping you from being on your path. But really they are there to allow you to express, for you to find your way to express and be and grow as a result of your being. Sometimes the darkness can be terrible, a terrible conflict, and so intensely dark it can be overwhelming, when everything is black, nothing is there, nothing can be seen or felt, there's a numbness, a fright, a fear. Step aside from this, let it go and come back to the light of yourself, the light of the strength of yourself, your spirit, don't become overwhelmed by external things but if this happens, find a quiet moment, even in a black moment of despair, to speak your truth, to yourself, to spirit, because they will know what it is you're facing . And they are waiting for this time, for when the quiet is enough for you to receive support they are waiting to give you, they want to give you, which will take you, out of the darkness, and as you come out of the darkness, there will be a change of energy in you, a difference in you, growth, of strength and determination, new ideas, and inspiration. And with these new resources that appeared because you've managed to pull yourself away from the dark, listen quietly to your spirit, your authentic self and allow spirit to help.

The resources, now grown in your Spring, to take you further, they will take you further, into a new blossoming, a new blossoming of empowerment and purpose. Next time, there is no hope, there is no way through, take your mind to somewhere else, take your mind to the trees and nature, feel the ground under your body, your feet and breathe in the energy of spirit around you and just be, with that energy. Allow it to filter out negativity, allow it to filter in the light, that will awaken your spirit, you will awaken your own spirit, and feel that resonance and support, and love, the warmth and the love, that spirit has for you.

Chapter Ten

Hello Shadow

At the tree with my power animals hoisting me up, sliding up the branches like a cat, leaping onto the cliff, running round like on four legs, into the cave, hopping into the cave onto a rock. "Welcome" he says as he stirs a cauldron.

Do you see how the ripples are created as I'm stirring this broth in the pot, a small movement just a small movement a shift of energy can create action in different directions that didn't exist before. The small movements that you make actually motivate, generate, a whole new, process of manifestation. You create action with a different intention, with each intention you make the action is different, the results are different, the end result is different. The effect that each process has creates a different solution, a very different solution to each other. And with that in mind, consider the actions that you take in the world, and then look at what is manifesting around you in your life, what is there that, that you can identify as being there as a result of your actions? When you really look, the answer will be everything. Everything around you is a result, is a direct result of what you've done, what you have thought, what you have intended. So in order to alter or improve or change what there is around you in your life, you need to apply a different intent, a different action, different thoughts, not staying with the same, just step aside and think again, look again, examine, what could be done to change what is there around you?

The situation, your condition, your environment, your being, and it's starts with your being, it starts with that inner, self, listening to that innerself, and allowing that voice to direct you to the action that will bring about the change that you want. And just that simple interaction with yourself, it's simple but it's difficult, because it takes a lot of trust, and belief that the voice you hear, is offering the support that you needt, particularly when suggestions are so different to what has been. This is the beauty of the power within all of us, the immense power that each of us contains and which is available to us all can show us if we listen and trust and believe, that the action we can take to change our situation, alter our life, manifest what we desire, all those things, are available to us, because of the power we hold within us if we know how to use that power, if we know that we have that power. This is not just to know something, it's a deep knowing, a deep knowing and trusting, belief, it's a strong belief. So no matter what the structures around us try to do to put us off or shake our belief, as long as we hold that, the strength within us the power within us increases and we will find that we are able to adapt and change and discover new possibilities, experience new directions, events, and manifestations that didn't exist at all in our world in the actions we had been taking up until that point. So when we feel stuck, confused, frustrated or worried about the way our life is playing out and can't see a solution to the difficulties or problems that are surrounding us, we need to step back from them and observe, be like an observer of your own life.

Step aside from the reality you are facing as if you are advising or supporting someone else with objectively creative rational thoughts that might open up an awareness of new, unexpected, possibilities. It's because your not bogged down or restricted by the events that are surrounding you, it's like a fresh slate a clean slate, looking at your life with a clean slate, almost like a new beginning. At the same time as listening to yourself, being present with yourself, and that presence will create the ripple effect, into a new direction, carrying your intention as you apply a different action, to bring about great change, to bring about abundance in different forms that didn't exist before. And it's this belief in your own power, this can be so empowering, positive and fulfilling to begin to fully engage and be present with yourself, and aware of your potential and where and how you can use it.

A flow of creative thoughts and ideas will emerge leading you to the solution that fits and resonates with you. And your life shifts, your life shifts into a new direction, new experiences, but your inner self, your connection with your inner self has changed too. You are no longer separate, you are working together to support and guide each other along the path, that was laid out before you before you arrived here in this life.

Knowing this, knowing these things, changes you, it changes your outlook, your attitude, your emotional and health because you know that within you you have the power and support of your spirit and the universe that wants only the best for you. It wants only for you to become aware of your potential and fulfill it in your creative ideas and thoughts whichever direction they may take you, whichever area suits you.

Everytime we look, around, and see people worrying about, engaged in their own process, their own life, their own path, you cannot judge them you cannot be judgemental because we are all on our own way at different stages of our own path, so there is different awareness, different attitudes and processes. And each person has an individual choice, their own choice to make, to listen and trust in the power that they hold and take that trust as far as they choose to. And it is the same for you, you have a choice, you have a choice to change, it takes courage, to run constantly into the unknown. But knowing we are supported by our spirit and the universe is the most empowering and fulfilling way to be, and the rewards, the rewards of that work of trust and belief are great, because they will always support and resonate and become your truth. So next time you are stirring your pot, be aware of your action, your intention, your desire, and allow them to combine together to work together, to bring about the change you seek, and manifest the abundance, that is waiting as a result of your trust, your belief, because of the power that you hold within you.

Chapter Eleven

Remembering Where You Came From

Immediately onto Eagles back, and above the base of the tree with the other animals standing by, watching as I go and fly into the darkness although there's light coming from a source somewhere, it's not entirely dark. The light is coming from the cave, from Merlin's cave, a glowing white light coming from the cave entrance. We settle down onto the ledge, Eagle nods, I smile and go in. There's a sensation somewhere in my body from the light, the energy in the room.

Merlin is there, it's like the whole place is Merlin, he says, "Did you feel that?"

Did you feel that sensation, that power running through your body as you entered the light which you were drawn to so strongly? The attraction was more than just superficial, a power, source, your spirit drawing you towards it, overriding any mind chatter you may have had, somewhere deep within you knew, that this place was where you need to be, although the reason was unclear, perhaps. But in answering the call of your spirit, allowing, the resonance that your spirit had with the place or experience or event that was taking place even though there was no particular rational explanation for why. For a time then you dropped into, a perfect resonance with yourself, you allowed that resonance to take place and you trusted it, believed in it, but more than a belief, a knowing a deep knowing within you, knew that, you had to be in this place, you had to go to this place, you had to do this thing, whatever the practical element of it was. But how many times in your life have you felt that way, a true deep, knowing of your truth?

The practice of this, is what you're here to develop and experience what happens. With the development of this inner gift, this communication with your authentic self your spirit, your essence will drive you into places, will bring about abundance, empowerment and development, a subtle deep inner development, a connection with who you are, who you truly are. What an exciting prospect, what an amazing adventure it will be for you. Awareness is the key, awareness of your body how it resonates, how it changes, maybe your breathing changes, perhaps there's a vibration deep in your abdomen or somewhere in your body telling you, urging you to follow through with whatever presents itself, with whatever is presenting itself, and causing this effect on your spirit, which then manifests as the physical sensation in your body. It's powerful, it's a powerful thing this energy connection with yourself, it's a strong powerful energy contained within your body, the shell of your body. So pay attention to your body, how does it react in different situations? What do you feel within your body at different times, or situations? Perhaps there is fear or joy, pleasure, anxiety, sadness, concern, exhaustion.

Each emotion will provide a clue, in your body for you to observe, be aware of and to react, appropriately. These signs are important to observe, your body is a key to the emotions held within your body, and the sensations are telling you, how your spirit feels, how your authentic self is feeling about a particular situation. Choosing to ignore or not pay attention to these sensations, may not be life threatening, it maybe, but it may not be but there may be clues that are being missed that would lead you into a happier place a more fulfilled place in your life.

Or perhaps they might just be clues or cues for remembering something that you had forgotten, and recognising them will help, or will remind you of a particular thing that is important. You have this amazing mechanism within your body, which is sending signals to you all the time, wanting to help and communicate, communicate with and support you in this life. The more you are aware of the signals and cues, the deeper the connection you will have with your authentic self, your essence, and the deeper that connection becomes, the more trust you will have, in the communications that it puts out to you.

It's a two way alignment, your body and spirit, your mind and your spirit, and your spirit is channelling information from the energy beyond our bodies, filtering in information, more and more information, as you are ready to receive it, it presents itself because you are ready to receive it. It is important to honour this presence within which is only here to help us, guide us, support us in the journey that will be for our highest good.

What a great resource to carry around with us, as we battle through our life, we battle throughout the ups and downs, the daily routines and habits and problems we encounter. And we look for help in a thousand different ways when the greatest help available to us, is being carried by us in the same body that is asking for help, so turn your attention inward in times of need, and in times that are good, turn your awareness inward and honour the presence of the power of spirit within you, within your body. That power is you, that power is your authentic self, it is who you are.

Sometimes, it can be very difficult to maintain, a strong link with spirit, and yourself because of the mind chatter that goes on, and on, particularly when there are stressful things happening, and this is the time that you need that connection the most, this nurturing, supporting, deeply loving resource that is always available. It does not want the suffering that you are encountering to continue, it wants you to step aside from that and dwell in the support that exists within you, not in the illusory problems that surround you. They are temporary, they are temporary and everything changes in life, good things come and go, not such good things come and go, but the one thing that doesn't come and go, is your spirit, your truth. The love of the source of life, which is within you and feeds, nurtures, and holds you in it's embrace, is the most powerful ally and resource you can have. It will overide, it will overide the darkness, the more, you become aware of the light that constantly shines within you. You will grow, you will discern the events that are happening in your life, and let go, be able to let go of the energies that are not supporting. You will discern the good energies, your body will feel those good energies and it will give you the signs for you to move in the right directon. It will lead you, to the light, the light of the life that you have come here to lead for a short time, and as you move through this life, just know, that you are supported and loved by this powerful, most powerful resource, and all you need is awareness of it.

Chapter Twelve

Take Another Step Forward

On Eagles back, flying through the branches of the trees, landing at the entrance to the cave, by a bright light in the entrance, I go in into the glow, there's quite a bit of movement around, Merlin is dancing. I sit and watch the flickering shadows of his movement in the light of the ceiling, he says, "It's good to move, when was the last time you moved your body, uncontrollably without being selfconscious about what you were doing ?

Giving your body freedom to move, just allowing that movement, a moment of freedom in your body to release any stresses and tensions, freeing your mind from thoughts and problems just tuning in with your body and allowing it to move, being with it, embracing it, embracing the pure bliss of freedom. And as you move, with no thought, you are sinking further into yourself, becoming yourself allowing yourself to emerge in a blissful state of freedom. Tasting that richness, a pureness, of being, not constrained by any social entanglements or subconscious restrictions or fears, just being that space, enjoying that moment of freedom and deep connection with your spirit as it merges with your body, a fluid, unconfined bliss. Take this feeling to a different place, in your thinking, as your mind takes over and controls how you are in the world. Imagine a blissful state of fulfilment and empowerment, enjoyment and satisfaction that can be felt by allowing your mind to have the same freedom as your body, as your body flows and sways whichever direction it feels like going, whatever movement it feels like making, a natural flow, a perfectly natural flow.

If your mind could be like that, imagine how your life can be, a life full of fluid movement, not constrained by fear, of what should be, and what you should be doing, what you need to do, what you haven't done yet, what you must keep doing, what you must keep doing to maintain the framework, of your life, the framework that confines, that your fear embraces you with. Imagine what you would do, what you can achieve, what you could experience, embrace in your life if your mind had the same fluid movement as your body, or if you gave the same fluid movement to your mind as you can to your body. Allow, the pure expression, the pure expression of your desires, your gifts, your skills, your dreams, to flow whichever direction it may take you, just allowing them to take you wherever, the flow finds its way into the world.

It takes a lot of trust, it takes a lot of trust, when we are faced with the obstacles to our flow, to find a way round them and continue in the direction we want to go, because we don't know what's on the other side of that barrier, we don't know if it will take us, to a dark place, of failure, and problems, or a place of light, a place of light and fulfilment. We won't know until we make that choice, until we make the choice to move, and unblock the flow.

But in doing so, whichever way, opens up on our path, it is empowering, it is empowering because we have made the choice, it wasn't made for us. And whatever comes on the path to create further obstacles, we will have the desire, the resources, to maintain the flow because we have seen, and felt what that means, to be ourselves and our spirit, and we cannot go back, we cannot go back to that place of stuckness, a place of worry about where our life will lead us. You should stay where you are even though you are deeply frustrated and confined and your gifts and desires are buried in the fear of change? We cannot go back to that place once we have tasted the true meaning of freedom, the true meaning of our creative growth and meaning and purpose in this life. It is not our meaning and purpose in this life to stop, to stop our gifts, to stop having dreams, to stop allowing our dreams to manifest, to stop the flow of our essence, our spirit, our desires and needs, that is not our purpose.

Our purpose, is to continually allow the flow, is to continually allow fulfilment of our potential which can only be, if the freedom for it is there to express. And for the freedom to be, there must be no fear, there must be no fear in the outcome. The spirit of life will guide us along the way, and we will feel that guidance get stronger and stronger, the support will get stronger as we give ourselves to it, as we give ourselves to the flow of our life, and in return the universe will be there with unconditional love for our spirit, our body, our self, nurturing our path, guiding us through the lessons that may show up that may be challenging because there will always be challenges whether we remain stuck or whether we flow. There will always be challenges, but when we are flowing, we are empowered to overcome those challenges, we are supported to overcome those challenges. So when we hear that song in our heart, the song that needs to be expressed, you will sing it, you will sing the song of your spirit and the universe will echo back with support and love, and you will then live a life of freedom.

The alternative, is to stop being authentic, the alternative is to stop flowing and not allow the potential we carry within to fully express itself and create the world that is possible. We don't know what that is, we have the universe and our spirit to help us reach as far as we can go, as far as we can flow. And the more we let go of ourselves into the journey, the more we flow with unrestrained freedom and joy in our life.

The more fulfilment and bliss will be a part of our life, and we will know our truth, and be at one with our own spirit, the universe and the unconditional love that will flow into our life, as we give ourselves over to it.

So begin with that movement of your body, feel the

bliss of the energy flowing through your body and allow it to go wherever it feels naturally to move and then examine, how your life, is flowing.

Chapter Thirteen

The Magic Unfolds

*U*p on Eagles back, straight up, flying straight to the cave entrance, the light is shining out from it, and I go in, it feels quiet, I sit down, waiting. Merlin suddenly jumps into sight. It wasn't what you're expecting was it?

You were expecting everything to be the same as usual, and it always feels a bit strange when things change unexpectedly, it's a good time to, sit back and reassess, what the habits of your expectations are, and what happens to you when there is an interruption in the flow of them. If you can take the time to, be like an outsider to the events, or whatever is going on, just think about the difference the changes make, to how you are in the world. How they affect your perception of things, and which sometimes produce a chain of thinking that is quite different, an acceptance of things an acceptance of a different way of thinking, different way of approaching something. And when that happens, it's almost like a little seed inside you has started to sprout, a shift, a new perception on expectations that you have, the habits that you have, what you were expecting, because you were used to the same thing happening. But it's good to have these little jolts of change and not remain, on one track, on a single track. And once the momentum has started for acceptance of the change however small it might be, this momentum brings about further changes in your life.

It's one of the things that life is about, it's about not remaining, within one framework of being. It's about the exploring, expanding, growing and changing, maturing, so that all the little layers of healing of habits, expectations, all the little healings of, the conditioned behaviour in certain areas of your life, certain scenarios that recur, repeating behaviours, repeating attitudes, all these little changes bring about the healing of those conditioned behaviours, attitudes, thoughts, perceptions. And it brings about expansion of choices, a range of choices develop, so you decide, for yourself and make a decision about something, instead of being driven by subconscious conditioned behaviour. And when you are free from remaining in your habitual response or thoughts and patterns, once you're aware of their existence, the awareness brings, begins to bring about healing, and a wider sense of your own choice making being made. And then you begin to know yourself better, you come to know how you really feel about a situation, a scenario, a person perhaps, and that can be very enriching, very empowering, because you're standing in your power. At that moment you have the power to decide yourself, how you will react and respond, how you will perceive, what you will think.

A freshness will come about, a change of energy within will be present to give you clarity, to shift away from the old patterns with ease and move into a different direction of attitude, and perception and being. And with this new, level, of consciousness that is emerging now that the blocks have been healed, there is endless possibility of what could happen next in your life. You have the power to choose what that will be, you have the awareness to know that you have the power to choose what happens in your life, what you accept and reject and change or follow for a while, while other changes take place, before new changes appear possible for you. The angst, the frustration that can occur from being stuck in habitual patterns of behaviour and perception, attitudes, will disappear, and you may look back and remember how you felt, how frustrated you may have felt, how stuck you may have felt, how lonely you may have felt, how worried you may have felt in your life as a result of being stuck in old patterns.

But when those barriers are broken and healed, fragmented, no longer holding the power they once had, they will gradually fade, and as they fade there'll be a weakening also, of the energy of repeating, the same pattern of holding on, to something that was familiar or keeping you restricted from being fulfilled and happy in your life.

The more flexible you can become with the changes that happen in your life, the circumstances that manifest, the challenges that appear, the newness of things the strangeness of things, the fear of things, all these emotions, can be identified much more easily, allowing healing to take place for anything that is embedded in your being. This growth, this inner strength that is developing within you is bringing about increased freedom, increased freedom for you to experience, different ways and different thinking and allowing yourself to flow in the direction, that will serve your highest good, that will bring about all the teachings you are here to experience.

Allowing the creativity within us all, to be allowed to run free, and express itself fully without restriction, or narrowminded frameworks. As you allow that flow to happen and let go of the old framework of thoughts and habits allowing the new to come in and go without holding on, just like the ebb and flow of tides, moving in and out and choosing the ideas that pop up that flow in on the tide of your new consciousness, your new awareness of your own potential and ability and power.

This will then be the time, for you to really know yourself. All the time this is happening your connection with spirit, is deepening, your connection with your own spirit is deepening, your essence, your true self is emerging through you, through your mind and your heart, and in partnership with your spirit and yourself and the love and strength and support from the universe that is always there with you, you are capable of doing anything, that you wish to do. All the barriers and restrictions have been removed and faded, a new energy within you is waiting, for the next change, the next moment, where a different perception, a different thought, and way of thinking, can take you further.

Chapter Fourteen

Awareness Of Everything

Power animals are by the tree, again I get onto Eagles back, the power animals are cheering from below and waving. We arrive on the cliff edge at the entrance to the cave, and a light is flickering on the walls, it's not as bright as usual and I go in, it's very warm, there's a big fire roaring at the side of the cave, and I sit down and look up and see Merlin's face in the shadows, smiling, rubbing his hands together.

It's amazing isn't it, what can bring comfort and joy to life, simple things, like a good fire. It seems to blow away those ideas and thoughts, of negativity, like a warm glow wrapping itself around you. Some times we miss the simple things, the simple things that are important to us, that are important for really bringing ourselves back to ourselves, and what we really only need to sustain our body and our mind our spirit. We place so much emphasis and importance on gathering and improving, making better, getting a more up to date version and it can consume us, this unconscious mission, of continuing to, be unsatisfied with what we have, and what we have, becomes, always becomes not good enough, not enough. And this endless search, this endless feeding of our desires takes us away further, from what really matters, from really matters in the nourishment of our being.

It is very easy to judge, and complain, even get angry or depressed because we might not have the money to buy the things we desire, but we if don't have or we can't get them for whatever reason, is our life really affected is it really less than it would be otherwise? If you were to get those things that you desire, how long would it be before, the next object was on the list? and the next one, and the next one, an endless stream of getting the next thing. We came into this life with nothing, except our purpose our souls purpose, and our souls purpose wasn't about accumulating material goods, and finding ways in which we could purchase them, obtain them. That isn't a deep lesson in life, it's a shallow superficial way of finding fulfilment, of finding satisfaction and masking, that which we don't want to, encounter. The pain that we carry inside us from the experiences that we've had so far is buried deep within us and it cannot be substituted by buying the latest gadget, or decoration, or clothing. It cannot be because those things will be redundant soon and you will need new and more items to replace them, but the pain you carry, remains. The dark ness that has etched itself on our spirit, through the experiences and traumas that we have all had however big or small in our life has left it's mark on our spirit.

So instead of journeying outward to the sales, and shops and catalogues, it's time to journey inward and scratch the surface of that pain. And once you begin, to take notice of what really brings pleasure to you, the relevance of material things will slip away and they will lose their power and grip, and you will begin to be more discerning about your needs, and how to provide for them. You'll smile at the simplicity, of the things that can bring such joy and fulfilment, and feelings of worth. It's not the new designer label, and the pressure of its ownership that will bring this about, it is your ability to, come back to yourself, and strip away, the trappings, you carry with you, and allow your spirit, your intuition, your heart to guide you as you, change course slightly in your life, a course that will bring, appreciation and gratitude for the life that you have and the abundance in your life. We all have a life, of abundance and when we can become aware of it, we will know it and recognise it as such, the simplicity of things, the simplicity of a fire, good food and nourishment and shelter and clothing. And as we take that journey inward, it's a search for that truth, that we have never found in the materials things, that deep truth about ourself, who we are, really, who we are, and what we need, what we truly need to bring about, the satisfaction and happiness that we all crave.

We will find that happiness and fulfilment, within ourselves, because we came with it, we brought it with us to enable us to have the journey of this life, to sustain us on the journey of this life, and it is still there, stored away behind the layers that we have piled on top of it, from all the hurt that we've accumulated, from all the rejections, failures, traumas, disappointments we've encountered so far. But when we truly find ourself, in those dark moments of discovery, we begin to find the reason, the reasons for our, our outward show of being, that mask we have been wearing. And as it is slowly stripped away, the empowerment that that will bring us will begin a new process, a new episode in our life, which will enable us to move more freely through life, more able to accept the things that don't turn out as we expected, the strength to discern what truly brings us happiness and peace, and not to compromise what that is once it's been discovered. Because once we begin that inner journey, there will be no turning back, to the previous route of unfulfilment.

There's nothing wrong with material goods and games, of course not, but like everything in life, it is in the balance, it is the balance that will set us free, from being trapped and losing our way, giving away our power, giving away our choice and freedom ,which we believe we have, but that has been an illusion. Without the inner journey, the external world is an illusion, which will prevent us, if we allow it, from finding our way, the way that will bring us to the place of true freedom and choice

Chapter Fifteen

When It Feels Right, Do It

Flying up with Eagle but the other animals are climbing up the tree as well, and when I land, I'm at the entrance of the cave. Wolf, Bear Stag and Owl, Elephant are there, gathered around the entrance and peering into the cave. And as I go in I can hear music, I can just hear very faint music, harps, violins, and drum, very faint, as I go into the cave there's shadows of a figure dancing, dancing shadows across the roof of the cave, the walls of the cave, a big fire, shadows flickering around and music. Then Merlin appears, sits down smiling.

It's amazing how the soul can be fed, by doing simple things, simply by acknowledging, really acknowledging the soul, spirit within, and feeding it, actively feeding it, really looking after it and finding out what its needs are, and finding time, making time to include them, in the daily routines of life. And that acknowledgement, that gift of connection, partnership, with your spirit, will feed into the rest of your life, will feed into your enjoyment, and embracing the life that you lead, whatever you might be doing. So you have this resource within you, which has been well fed by giving it the opportunity, to play and to enjoy and be light, and have fun, and freedom to express. Small things, tokens really of acts of enjoyment, to freely express itself.

This resource that we are feeding, is our authentic self, and by giving it nourishment, it has the strength to tackle the challenges that come our way. And there is a lightness to our world, a lightness to our step because we know we are not alone, we aren't alone we are doing it in partnership with our spirit, whatever we are doing. And so it's important to recognise what those things are, that will bring this about, and to honour that time spent freely with our spirit as if it's being with a friend and going out and having a good time, have a good time with your spirit. Build a relationship, and in this relationship, there will be a great deal of support which you can call on any time, for advice, counselling, or just to be heard as problems or issues arise. And this amazing resource that is intrinsically who we are, has another relationship, a connection with the colossal bank of support and information that exists in the energy outside of our body. And so there is a direct link to that energy, to that resource, the information, advice and support and love. You are surrounded by it, you are immersed in it and it is available at any time.

There are beings, spirits, present in that energy whose energy resonates with ours, and who know the path we are taking, they know the reasons for us being here, they are aware of everything about us, what we need, what we are going through, what we wish to accomplish and what experiences we will have that will teach us the lessons we have come to learn. They know what we have experienced so far and know what we will experience in the future. They know the difficulties we face sometimes and the challenges, particularly the dark times. In times of darkness when it is is difficult see the light, beyond the challenge and your're consumed and overwhelmed by the challenge, it is then their support and guidance can be most valuable.

And the more we honour this connection that's available, the deeper the presence of this resource will be available to us along with the presence of the spirits who are waiting and available to us, offering with deep compassion and love, the support we ask for, the guidance that we ask for.

And so it is also important just as it's important to feed our spirit with lightness, to interact, with that other resource, those other beings, in a light loving way, with acknowledgement and honouring, feeling the presence around us, which in turn will strengthen, empower the resonance, the alignment, of these amazing resources. And by sharing our moments of joy with those beings of love, we can experience some moments of pleasure in their company, and really nurture the relationship that we have. And all these connections, will enable us in this life on Earth to walk with a lighter step. Be guided, listen, listen, hear the guidance that is being offered , leading to, leading to the light of life, through the darkness and the challenges that will always show up as lessons in life. But when we know there is always light, through the darkness, always light, and we are carried and supported, constantly towards it, we will overcome the challenges, we will not be overwhelmed, by the darkness, and we will find the light, shining in our life in our spirit, in our self. It will be like an armour around us, deflecting negativity, negative energy that can prevent us from taking the next step forward, very easily prevent us from taking the next step forward if we are not in our light but when we honour the nurtured relationship we have with our spirit, the resources and beings that walk with us, we will overcome, and be, the source of light

Chapter Sixteen

Follow Your Spirit

*T*he power animals are waiting at the base of the tree, they seem to be quite excited about me coming. We start racing each other up the tree, there's a lot of fun lightness and laughter going on trying to beat each other up the branches. Getting to the top, when I get there Wolf is there smiling, "beat you ", he said, "I knew I could do it", and he leads the way on the path to the cave entrance. Wolf is the only animal there now, he's walking around waiting for me to go in. I go into the cave and I'm struck by the silence, there's a palpable silence, it's very light, strongly lit but it's absolutely silent. It's almost as if I can feel the silence permeating my body, and I feel overcome by a deep feeling of peace as if all the cells of my body are relaxed and receiving this energy, this silence, this silence and energy. And Merlin comes into view, and it's almost like he's levitating slightly off the ground, gliding across the floor of the cave, playing with the energy thats there.

Silence, he says is a powerful thing, a powerful weapon, against the multitude, of distractions, that really assault our senses every day, and we are so used to receiving noise in different forms in our lives, it's not until we experience a complete silence, that we might not even be aware of that noise it's such a natural thing to us. And all that noise, all those sounds we encounter have a vibration a frequency, every sound every pitch every tone has a different vibration frequency. And our bodies which, vibrate with their own frequency receive this deluge, this deluge of discordant vibrations from the sounds around us, and without us even knowing, the sounds and tones, vibrations and frequencies which are discordant with our body, affect us.

On a physical level, and emotional level, mental level, spiritual level, all the levels of energy that we have are constantly being bombarded and it affects our physical health, our mental health, our spiritual health if we are unable to filter out, or avoid the frequencies and tones and sounds that can impact our well-being, some are obvious and some are not so obvious. The not so obvious come from the tones and vibrations of other people's voices, and how they interact and how we interact with them, different levels of speech, different intentions in the words create different vibrations and frequencies of energy that we receive. And so we can receive, the energy behind the words, behind the tones of the words, and if they are pleasant and friendly and come from a place of love, we receive that love, our body receives it, we hear it in the words but our body receives it in the vibration of the energy, and we feel good. It's good to interact, on that level and receive that energy, but if the intention, if the words and the intentions, the energy of these things, are harmful.

If there is anger or fear, jealousy, rage, judgement, criticism, then we receive the energy of those things too, it impacts our body, and we feel it, we feel it in our body, it impacts our well-being, it's like we are being attacked not just verbally but energetically. And if we are not strong in ourselves, standing in our power with a strong sense of self, a strong sense of who we are, what we want, then that energy can impact our body and our spirit. Gradually affecting our well-being, our physical well-being our mental well-being as that energy, that negative energy, resonates within us, eventually creating physical pain emotional stress, and a loss of spiritual power. We are surrounded by energy, moving all around us all the time, everything around us is emitting its own energy, it's own frequency of energy, and so it's important for us to recognise that and be aware of what makes us feel good and what makes us feel not so good.

Our body will feel the first signs as it receives the energy that is being emitted. And so we must take heed and notice what our body is telling us, how we feel, in the energy of the place that we're at, what we feel about the energy of the person we are interacting with, what is happening to us when we make a decision about something, or reply to something. Are we receiving an energy and responding in a discordant way that doesn't resonate with our true self? Does it cause, a reverberation within us that we can feel if we care to notice. A sign that our body, is giving us that the energy we are receiving is good or it's not so good for us to join with.

These periods of complete silence, is really about attuning yourself to your body, a silence of the mind creates that space in which we can tune into the silence of our body, and hear, what the silence has to say to us, because we carry a voice within us that can only be heard in the silence. The voice of our spirit which fills our body and knows, the right frequency, for our well-being our complete well-being and so it will create nudges within us vibrational nudges rippling through our body to indicate, excitement, joy, and also anxiety or fear, coherent and incoherent energy that we are experiencing, or even about to experience. That voice needs to be heard, so that we may fulfil, the wishes of our spirit and stay on the track it is guiding us to take.

So in those moments of deep silence, they are only silent from the outside world, because that voice within us will be given freedom to be louder and be heard. And when we are familiar with this voice, we will become more familiar with the energy that we need to avoid, energy that is bad or detrimental to our well-being and our path. It will then be clearer for us to follow and attach ourselves more to the energy of those things that resonate within us, because they are taking us on the path, they are leading us on the path, that will lead us, into the life and experiences that our higher self wishes to go, that we planned to go, the plan we made before arriving here. There'll be constant challenges of course, constant distractions, to take us away from our path, but we will be empowered and be strong, not allowing that other energy to absorb us, distract us, from our task, from our truth. The energy of our truth will always resonate, and we will begin to know the difference as we listen, as we begin to listen, to the silence.

Chapter Seventeen

Releasing and Changing

Power animals are running round the tree, Eagles flying about and waiting for me to arrive, and Eagle asks if I want to fly on it's back and Wolf wants me to go on it's back, I decide to go on the back of Wolf. And we're moving really quickly from branch to branch, leaping across the gaps and then leap onto the edge of the cliff and go round to the cave entrance . "I hope you enjoyed that", said Wolf, "yeah it was great", he says, "I hope your'e going to enjoy this", and I go into the cave which is brightly lit as usual. There's no figure, no Merlin there, there's a fire blazing, there's cups and things on the table, and I sit down looking at the fire. Merlin's face is in the fire and he steps out of the fire. He say's, "embrace, embrace the life that you have, it's a short time on Earth in this life."

Fully commit to your journey, find the route that will take you on the path that will, show you and help you manifest, the strengths that you have. Not only the strengths and the skills that you have in doing things and the ability to make things or do things and make things happen but the strength within you that will help you or enable you to continue during the tough times, challenges, the challenges that your strength faces. And in doing this, in really doing this and focusing, being aware and nurturing a power that you have within you to get you through, to get you through those times which seem impossible when your resources feel drained, your emotional energy your mental energy is drained, and you feel like you've just had enough, you don't want to continue with this path, you've been on this path all your life and it continues to be challenging. It continues to be hard, and you feel as if you just had enough and you want to be like everybody else, who seem to be enjoying life or getting through life, without too much deep analysis of who they are, maybe there's just too much deep analysis and not enough living going on.

This is the version that your mind creates for you,

your ego creates for you, your rational mind creates the scenarios that can convince you to stop, to stop on your path, right now where you are is the best thing you should do. And they try to convince you, that there is little point to continue pushing yourself, pushing yourself even though you are healing yourself at the same time, taking you further and stretching yourself to realise your potential your full potential. And that is the challenge, the big challenge of life, not to give up, not to stop being or allowing your authentic being, your spirit, to help you, help you, go as far as you can go in this life in this short life, a blink of an eye in the great scheme of things. But the challenge does not have to be continually difficult like a chore, a problem to be solved, a mission.

It's there so that you can take a light step from one stone to another, from one experience to another and see the connections between the two, how there was an invisible link joining them, it wasn't apparent or planned it just appeared, just in time, just in time for the next step to manifest. And if you look back and see the steps that you have taken to be where you are right now, all those pieces that appeared out of the blue to help create that series of steps, you'll begin to see, you'll perhaps begin to see, the pattern the support and the desire of spirit for you to go as far as you can. Sometimes in that darkness, that darkness of sadness, of loneliness, of fear, anxiety and loss, there can be a great loss, a great feeling of loss, and failure, as the path continues, making you think it continues because you failed, so far you have failed and therefore it continues. But that is not the case, that is not the case, you have been open, it continues because you are open to the reality of your path and what it takes to continue along it. And in those dark lonely times, that feeling of being alone in the world, and lost, is when the greatest temptation to stop appears.

But when we remember the guidance that we've had so far the support that we've had so far, and be aware of the support that is still with us, the guidance and the love that is still with us. Spirit, is available to us in nature, the visible face of spirit and if we look there we will receive, a new wave, a new surge of strength, a new surge of confidence, a new surge of knowing what we must do. All it takes is to be open, open our hearts, scream, cry, or just ask, if we cry with an open heart to spirit, bare ourselves to spirit in those dark times and plead and ask for help, it will come, it will be there, and we will feel it's energy within us. And we will know, what our next step will be and we will feel comfortable with that and we will know that we are capable of it, and that that is all we need to do next and we will know, because we have received a direct link, a direct link from spirit, a clear insight of what that step should be, and we will have the resources to see it through. We will be uplifted and empowered and step out of the shadow that contained us for a short time, step out of the shadow and stride purposefully with a lightness of step, further along our path further to manifesting what we desire what our heart desires what our spirit desires.

For our spirit knows what is waiting for us, it knows because, it came with the entire plan, the entire plan of our life, but we have forgotten that and so we must trust in our spirit, it is a trust in our own spirit, awareness of our own spirit, that will enable us to fulfil that plan. And knowing this we can then enjoy the changes that take place in our life, because each change creates the energy, the next component of what that plan, is about and what it is going to achieve for you, what it is going to bring to you. But all the way along the route it is bringing you things, it is bringing you all kinds of things, gifts strengths, healings of past pain and conditioning, because all those things must happen in order to be clear and strong and have the resources to take you to the end of your path into the light of abundance, success and continued growth. So in the next dark moment, the next time of despair, reach out to spirit reach out to spirit with your heart, and it will be there, to hold your hand and lead you back into the light.

Chapter Eighteen

Holding The Past

There's a light around the tree and around the power animals gathered there, they're bathed in a white light and I look up through the tree as the white light spreads further up the branches higher and higher, and I feel myself engulfed in white light, and I levitate up through the branches spiralling around the branches and floating and land directly outside the cave of Merlin. I look down at myself and I'm still engulfed in a white light, my body is immersed in a white light or just is a white light, and I go in almost gliding across the floor, the cave is filled with a white light and there are other figures there as well, other white figures, and Merlin appears, his face appears in the white light.

"Healing," he says, healing, a big component of what this life is about. If we were immersed in this white light, white healing light for our entire life we would be protected from any negative energy, but we're not, we don't have this armour to protect us through our life, but what we do have, is the power within us, to go forward and deal with whatever comes our way. So in itself this power is the healing armour too, it's just not a visible protection, but it is a powerful piece in the armoury available to us, as we go through our life. We can quickly lose the sense and awareness of this power through the conditioning and influence we receive when we are young and we forget we have it and we believe we are powerless, in this life. We just have ourselves, to get us through problems of everyday life along with our families and friends who are there but who also carry the same sense of being powerless.

The energy of the universe has colossal strength and power, it is constantly creating, expanding, and we are catalysts for that expansion and creativity, the more you expand and create, the more the universe expands and the more knowledge is available. So we therefore have a direct link, with this energy, we are not only adding to it, but we can use it to help us, guide us, support us, empower us. And when we know we have this connection, this resource and that it is available at any moment, at every moment, a constant healing armour available to us, we can begin to address and to heal the wounds that we carry within us. If we ask to be directed to the source of our pain, and then go deep within ourselves and find the source of that pain or trauma, we may be surprised to see what the source of that pain actually was. A source that may have seemed so irrelevant, a minor experience, but somehow has caused such long-standing, long lasting pain and influence on our attitudes and beliefs and behaviours throughout our life.

An incident that has caused our life to be the way it has been, but when we access that source and the armour of the universe the energy, the healing energy of the universe to remove that negative energy from us, to heal the pain and the wounds that we carry, we have deepened the connection of our energy and what is available to to us. In trusting and acknowledging that it is available for healing ourselves, we can also use it to create and manifest great things in our life. Whatever it is we might want or desire can be made available by using the power of the energy of the universe, by asking, and then trusting that it will do it's work.

You're not taught to trust deeply in things that don't exist in a physical presence, not to believe in something we know nothing about without evidence to back it up. But when we can experience the healing power of the energy, allow ourselves to trust the simplicity of this communication and become aware of the possibilities that can be open to us, the more we expand our awareness and trust. And as we do so, this armour, this healing armour of spirit will be more present and strengthen the belief in our self to embrace the power within us and know that we are not walking this path through life, alone.

The universe, is a collosal bank of information, and by engaging with this energy through nature ,through an open heart, a deep belief of it's existence, anything is possible, anything and everything is possible. So we walk this life, and when we walk this life knowing, not just believing but knowing that we have this protection, this healing armour around us, we can embrace the experiences that unfold, embrace everything that unfolds in our life knowing that whatever happens, we have the power within to remain, our authentic self. To truly be our authentic self and not be carried away and influenced by that which may cause negativity or pain, we can deflect the pain, we can deflect negativity and embrace the positivity and joy that is present in everything around us even though it can sometimes be masked, by others pain, the pain of others, the negativity of others. If we feel this affecting us we can call on spirit, reconnect our energy and re charge the batteries of positive energy and resources of spirit, we no longer have to suffer, we are not in this life to suffer, we are in this life to create and add to the wonderful beauty of this life.

We all have that possibility within us, so embrace your self, embrace your life, and the power that's around you, and walk tall along your path. And as you do so, with a confidence, a lightness and joy in your step, others will notice the light shining from you, others who walk in darkness, will see your light, and wish to know from where it comes. It's the responsibility of all those who walk in their light, to share their light and show how others may do so, those who walk in darkness. And in doing so, we are sharing the love of spirit with others who need it and who perhaps don't yet know they need it, just as spirit and the universe is sharing their love with you, throughout your life.

Chapter Nineteen

Embrace Your Life

The power animals are there vaguely but the tree seems to have changed shape it's much bigger, it's kind of split into different branches coming from thick trunks coming from the earth. And I have to choose one to go up, which route to take, and I take the right, the right branch, and it's bending over it's arched, bending over and I'm walking along it almost like a tightrope walker as it bends with my weight, and as I get further along it's bent right over now arched, there's a shake in the tree and it flips me off into the air like a catapult, and I'm flying up into nothing, and I actually land on the cliff right outside the cave of Merlin, and I look behind, so surprised at the entrance that I've made. I go into the cave which has the light coming from it as usual, but it's quite dim as well, I'm feeling myself along the walls of the cave and I come to a sort of annex which I haven't seen before, there's a seat a stone seat, I sit down, almost in the shadows of the cave looking out at the other part which is lit , strange. Merlin's feet appear walking into the light as I look down, and he points to the line thats running across the floor of the cave the line between the light and the dark.

He said it's a thin line, between walking in shadow and not knowing who you are fully, and being in the light, and knowing yourself, knowing who you really are, who you really are, and being that person, living your life living your authenticity, knowing, that you are on a path. There is no getting away from that, you can hide, hide in the shadows of denial and illusion and have contempt for those who seek the light, contempt because you have doubt that it exists.

The life lead in the shadow supplies an illusion of what your life is really about, and who you are. This is the crucial piece, it is about finding out, but not just that but really seeking to know. But you can only do that when you know that you have that right, that power, to be your authentic self and to question, what the shadow is showing you, what life it is giving you.

It takes a lot of courage, to really ask those questions, because the dark side the shadow side, is the illusion is that you know, it's what you know to be your truth, your identity. This restriction and denial suppresses any interest, any possibility of the reality, that is there for you to embrace. We carry so much pain with us, we carry so many conditioned beliefs about ourselves, there is little space to allow the light to shine in, into our spirit, into our world, into our reality of life.

But, my friend, this work is all about asking you, to embrace, a possible new beginning for yourself, to embrace the power that you have that you carry within you of your individuality, your potential, and the impact that your life can make, by accepting, the truth of who you, the truth of your life, and what is possible.

So many people live in the shadow of their life, accepting the restrictions, the frameworks that have developed within themselves, and the denial and doubt, that keeps, that keeps that denial strong, and the ability to justify, very easily, reasons for staying in the shadow. Reasons to not look beyond, to not be open to something different something different that will give meaning to existence, to give meaning to this time that you are here, that will lead you to discovering, why you are here this time and not some other time.

Ask why you have had the life that you've had, and how you can change it, so that the plans that your spirit, your authentic self made before you were born, can be realised and change the shape of your reality. If you can allow a crack, a chink of light of curiosity to enter the shadow, it will begin the change for you, it will open up new directions new chains of thought, new ideas for yourself. And the light will gradually move, move across the line of the shadow, until the shadow starts to recede, and the light begins to fill the remainder of your life. You're only here for a short time, everything alive has a cycle of life and that includes you.

It doesn't matter how late in life the light starts to shine, the important thing is, that it has been allowed access, and will be able to impact, your life, whatever time the crack appears because you will be ready at that time, to receive, the energy and changes that it brings in it's path. We are all at different stages in our lives to receive the light, to spend time in the shadow is important too because the experiences and lessons that we've had during that time have lead us to this place now. Looking beyond the shadow, seeking, a different way of being, but that is only possible when we are ready to do so.

This work is about, helping that process, an introduction to making that step and what it can bring for you, what it can lead to the more steps that you take, in the light.

It is my honour, to speak to you, it's my deep privilege, to speak to you, these words, this information.

Chapter Twenty

No Fear Or Regret, Trust!

The power animals are at the tree and dancing around very excited, shouting "come on, come on," this is great, and I go towards them and they gather round, they're jumping about, running about, dancing about. And one says, "come on we've got to go, we have a visitor to go and see for the last time, for now". And we all slide up the tree, snaking up the tree, like a cat up the branches on it's belly, and we get to the cliff edge and there are lights on the path, all the way along the path to the entrance of the cave where a bright light is shining.

The power animals hang back a bit and push me forward , "go on, go on", they said, and I step forward and go towards the cave, crouching down into the entrance which is smaller than usual for some reason and I have to crouch down to get into it.

Down some steps it's a little bit different, into a sunken floor, it's quite dark yet there's a bright light above it, and I sit down in this dark space looking up at the edges where the light starts, and Merlin comes to the edge. He's dressed in his finery, robes and wearing a kind of crown, holding a staff, carrying a staff an elaborate wooden staff with crystals embedded in it. He stands at the edge and just looks down at me, his voice seems to boom around the cave.

"NOW", *he says,*
"NOW, NOW YOU KNOW, YOU KNOW WHAT IT TAKES TO LIVE A GOOD LIFE, ON EARTH"

You know what it takes to find that way, to be that person that resonates with your spirit. That is all that this work is about, finding that way to resonate with your spirit. We've talked about awareness a lot, awareness of your spirit and awareness of the power that you carry within you, that you've always carried within you waiting for your awareness to give it life, to give it the life, that you came to experience. You know about the energy connection that is constantly available to you at any time for help and guidance and support, that walks with you constantly, has always been there and will always be there. So we've talked about these things, and now it's time for you to step into a new life, a new life filled with hope, not just a hope but a knowing, optimism, a knowing that you are not alone on your journey and a knowing that you have a purpose to fulfill in your time here.

The belief that you will carry with you about your true nature, the possibilities that exist for you, the guidance and support that you can call on at any time, and that the more you trust in that guidance and support the more abundant your life will become in many ways, the more fulfilling more empowering it will become. So there is no need any longer for you to sit in the dark, the darkness of frustration, hopelessness and of being lost not knowing your purpose, not knowing what life, what this life for you is about, giving your power away, and being power less . These things are in the past and the timing of this work arrived to you, because the universe is telling you that it is now your time, it is now your time to change and constantly walk in the light. And when the challenges of life appear, you will have the resources to overcome them and not be overwhelmed by the problems that you'll face, and each time a problem is beaten your resources will grow stronger. So look in the mirror at yourself, look into your eyes, through your eyes into your soul and connect with your spirit, connect, with the life of that which is inside your body, not in your mind, look into your heart and hear what it is telling you, and feel that resonance and acceptance and energy, uplifting inspiring you to manifest and be your truth in your actions and in the words you speak .

May they carry your power, your intention, your truth, your spirit.
It has been my pleasure, a great pleasure in finding this route to bring these words to you at this time. It has been difficult to, find the time, to wait for the time, when these words will have the most impact for you, but having found them here, the universe has guided you to find them just as the universe has guided the words to come in this way at this time. The universe is constantly providing signs and omens, nudges to help you find your path your way in life and now it has provided this omen, in words that can be re-read over and over. And as you do so, may the spirit that lies behind them, rest in your heart and give you strength and love as you step forward

empowered, inspired, into the light.

My name is Merlin, and Martin was chosen, to receive these words and spread them into the world, into your world, just as you have been chosen at this time to receive them.
They are a gift to you from the universe, and may you honour and bless the life that you have on Earth from now on.

And when the time is right, we will meet again.
My Friends, I Wish You Well, Enjoy, Your Time, Embrace This Time, Have No Regrets No Fear.

Trust.

Thats All You Need My Friend,

Thats The Work